GW00630778

Francis Frith's
VICTORIAN & EDWARDIAN
KENT

◆

PHOTOGRAPHIC MEMORIES

Francis Frith's

VICTORIAN & EDWARDIAN
KENT

◆

Keith Howell

First published in hardback in the United Kingdom in 2000 by
The Francis Frith Collection®

Hardback edition 2000
ISBN 1-85937-149-3

Paperback edition 2002
ISBN 1-85937-624-X

Reprinted in paperback 2006

Text and Design copyright The Francis Frith Collection®
Photographs copyright The Francis Frith Collection® except where indicated.

The Frith® photographs and the Frith® logo are reproduced under licence from
Heritage Photographic Resources Ltd, the owners of the Frith® archive and trademarks.
'The Francis Frith Collection', 'Francis Frith' and 'Frith' are registered trademarks of
Heritage Photographic Resources Ltd.

All rights reserved. No photograph in this publication may be sold to a third party other than in the
original form of this publication, or framed for sale to a third party. No parts of this publication may be
reproduced, stored in a retrieval system, or transmitted, in any form, or by any means, electronic, mechanical,
photocopying, recording or otherwise, without the prior permission of the publishers and copyright holder.

British Library Cataloguing in Publication Data

Victorian & Edwardian Kent Photographic Memories
Keith Howell
ISBN 1-84589-624-X

The Francis Frith Collection®
Frith's Barn, Teffont,
Salisbury, Wiltshire SP3 5QP
Tel: +44 (0) 1722 716 376
Email: info@francisfrith.co.uk
www.francisfrith.com

Printed and bound in Great Britain

Front Cover: Sandgate, High Street 1906 56952t

The colour-tinting is for illustrative purposes only, and is not intended to be historically accurate

Every attempt has been made to contact copyright holders of illustrative material.
We will be happy to give full acknowledgement in future editions for any items not credited.
Any information should be directed to The Francis Frith Collection®.

AS WITH ANY HISTORICAL DATABASE THE FRITH ARCHIVE IS CONSTANTLY BEING CORRECTED AND IMPROVED
AND THE PUBLISHERS WOULD WELCOME INFORMATION ON OMISSIONS OR INACCURACIES

Contents

FRANCIS FRITH: *Victorian Pioneer*

FRANCIS FRITH, Victorian founder of the world-famous photographic archive, was a complex and fascinating man. A devout Quaker and a highly successful Victorian businessman, he was both philosophical by nature and pioneering in outlook.

By 1855 Francis Frith had already established a wholesale grocery business in Liverpool, and sold it for the astonishing sum of £200,000, which is the equivalent today of over £15,000,000. Now a very rich man, he was able to indulge his passion for travel. As a child he had pored over travel books written by early explorers, and his fancy and imagination had been stirred by family holidays to the sublime mountain regions of Wales and Scotland. 'What lands of spirit-stirring and enriching scenes and places!' he had written. He was to return to these scenes of grandeur in later years to 'recapture the thousands of vivid and tender memories', but with a different purpose. Now in his thirties, and captivated by the new science of photography, Frith set out on a series of pioneering journeys to the Nile regions that occupied him from 1856 until 1860.

INTRIGUE AND ADVENTURE

He took with him on his travels a specially-designed wicker carriage that acted as both dark-room and sleeping chamber. These far-flung journeys were packed with intrigue and adventure. In his life story, written when he was sixty-three, Frith tells of being held captive by bandits, and of fighting 'an awful midnight battle to the very point of surrender with a deadly pack of hungry, wild dogs'. Sporting flowing Arab costume, Frith arrived at Akaba by camel sixty years before Lawrence, where he encountered 'desert princes and rival sheikhs, blazing with jewel-hilted swords'.

During these extraordinary adventures he was assiduously exploring the desert regions bordering the Nile and patiently recording the antiquities and peoples with his camera. He was the first photographer to venture beyond the sixth cataract. Africa was still the mysterious 'Dark Continent', and Stanley and Livingstone's historic meeting was a decade into the future. The conditions for picture taking confound belief. He laboured for hours in his wicker dark-room in the sweltering heat of the desert, while the volatile chemicals fizzed dangerously in their trays. Often he was forced to work in remote tombs and caves where conditions were cooler. Back in London he exhibited his photographs and was 'rapturously cheered' by members of the Royal Society. His reputation as a photographer was made overnight. An eminent modern historian has likened their impact on the population of the time to that on our own generation of the first photographs taken on the surface of the moon.

VENTURE OF A LIFE-TIME

Characteristically, Frith quickly spotted the opportunity to create a new business as a specialist publisher of photographs. He lived in an era of immense and sometimes violent change. For the poor in the early part of Victoria's reign work was a drudge and the hours long, and people had precious little free time to enjoy themselves. Most had no

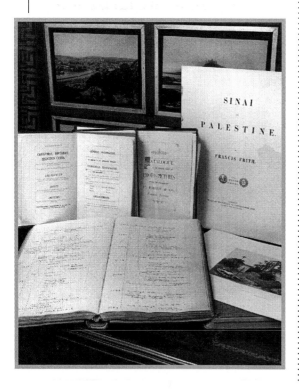

transport other than a cart or gig at their disposal, and had not travelled far beyond the boundaries of their own town or village. However, by the 1870s, the railways had threaded their way across the country, and Bank Holidays and half-day Saturdays had been made obligatory by Act of Parliament. All of a sudden the ordinary working man and his family were able to enjoy days out and see a little more of the world.

With characteristic business acumen, Francis Frith foresaw that these new tourists would enjoy having souvenirs to commemorate their days out. In 1860 he married Mary Ann Rosling and set out with the intention of photographing every city, town and village in Britain. For the next thirty years he travelled the country by train and by pony and trap, producing fine photographs of seaside resorts and beauty spots that were keenly bought by millions of Victorians. These prints were painstakingly pasted into family albums and pored over during the dark nights of winter, rekindling precious memories of summer excursions.

THE RISE OF FRITH & CO

Frith's studio was soon supplying retail shops all over the country. To meet the demand he gathered about him a small team of photographers, and published the work of independent artist-photographers of the calibre of Roger Fenton and Francis Bedford. In order to gain some understanding of the scale of Frith's business one only has to look at the catalogue issued by Frith & Co in 1886: it

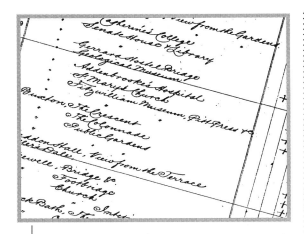

runs to some 670 pages, listing not only many thousands of views of the British Isles but also many photographs of most European countries, and China, Japan, the USA and Canada – note the sample page shown above from the hand-written *Frith & Co* ledgers detailing pictures taken. By 1890 Frith had created the greatest specialist photographic publishing company in the world, with over 2,000 outlets – more than the combined number that Boots and WH Smith have today! The picture on the right shows the *Frith & Co* display board at Ingleton in the Yorkshire Dales (left of window). Beautifully constructed with a mahogany frame and gilt inserts, it could display up to a dozen local scenes.

POSTCARD BONANZA

The ever-popular holiday postcard we know today took many years to develop. In 1870 the Post Office issued the first plain cards, with a pre-printed stamp on one face. In 1894 they allowed other publishers' cards to be sent through the mail with an attached adhesive halfpenny stamp. Demand grew rapidly, and in 1895 a new size of postcard was permitted called the court card, but there was little room for illustration. In 1899, a year after Frith's death, a new card measuring 5.5 x 3.5 inches became the standard format, but it was not until 1902 that the divided back came into being, with address and message on one face and a full-size illustration on the other. *Frith & Co* were in the vanguard of postcard development, and Frith's sons Eustace and Cyril continued their father's monumental task, expanding the number of views offered to the public and recording more and more places in Britain, as the coasts and countryside were opened up to mass travel.

Francis Frith died in 1898 at his villa in Cannes, his great project still growing. The archive he created continued in business for another seventy years. By 1970 it contained over a third of a million pictures of 7,000 cities, towns and villages. The massive photographic record Frith has left to us stands as a living monument to a special and very remarkable man.

Frith's Archive: *A Unique Legacy*

FRANCIS FRITH'S legacy to us today is of immense significance and value, for the magnificent archive of evocative photographs he created provides a unique record of change in 7,000 cities, towns and villages throughout Britain over a century and more. Frith and his fellow studio photographers revisited locations many times down the years to update their views, compiling for us an enthralling and colourful pageant of British life and character.

We tend to think of Frith's sepia views of Britain as nostalgic, for most of us use them to conjure up memories of places in our own lives with which we have family associations. It often makes us forget that to Francis Frith they were records of daily life as it was actually being lived in the cities, towns and villages of his

day. The Victorian age was one of great and often bewildering change for ordinary people, and though the pictures evoke an impression of slower times, life was as busy and hectic as it is today.

We are fortunate that Frith was a photographer of the people, dedicated to recording the minutiae of everyday life. For it is this sheer wealth of visual data, the painstaking chronicle of changes in dress, transport, street layouts, buildings, housing, engineering and landscape that captivates us so much today. His remarkable images offer us a powerful link with the past and with the lives of our ancestors.

TODAY'S TECHNOLOGY

Computers have now made it possible for Frith's many thousands of images to be accessed almost instantly. In the Frith archive today, each photograph is carefully 'digitised' then stored on a CD Rom. Frith archivists can locate a single photograph amongst thousands within seconds. Views can be catalogued and sorted under a variety of categories of place and content to the immediate benefit of researchers. Inexpensive reference prints can be created for them at the touch of a mouse button, and a wide range of books and other printed materials assembled and published for a wider, more general readership - in the next twelve months over a hundred Frith local history titles will be published! The

See Frith at www. francisfrith.com

day-to-day workings of the archive are very different from how they were in Francis Frith's time: imagine the herculean task of sorting through eleven tons of glass negatives as Frith had to do to locate a particular sequence of pictures! Yet the archive still prides itself on maintaining the same high standards of excellence laid down by Francis Frith, including the painstaking cataloguing and indexing of every view.

It is curious to reflect on how the internet now allows researchers in America and elsewhere greater instant access to the archive than Frith himself ever enjoyed. Many thousands of individual views can be called up on screen within seconds on one of the Frith internet sites, enabling people living continents away to revisit the streets of their ancestral home town, or view places in Britain where they have enjoyed holidays. Many overseas researchers welcome the chance to view special theme selections, such as transport, sports, costume and ancient monuments.

We are certain that Francis Frith would have heartily approved of these modern developments, for he himself was always working at the very limits of Victorian photographic technology.

THE VALUE OF THE ARCHIVE TODAY

Because of the benefits brought by the computer, Frith's images are increasingly studied by social historians, by researchers into genealogy and ancestory, by architects, town planners, and by teachers and schoolchildren involved in local history projects. In addition, the archive offers every one of us a unique opportunity to examine the places where we and our families have lived and worked down the years. Immensely successful in Frith's own era, the archive is now, a century and more on, entering a new phase of popularity.

THE PAST IN TUNE WITH THE FUTURE

Historians consider the Francis Frith Collection to be of prime national importance. It is the only archive of its kind remaining in private ownership and has been valued at a million pounds. However, this figure is now rapidly increasing as digital technology enables more and more people around the world to enjoy its benefits.

Francis Frith's archive is now housed in an historic timber barn in the beautiful village of Teffont in Wiltshire. Its founder would not recognize the archive office as it is today. In place of the many thousands of dusty boxes containing glass plate negatives and an all-pervading odour of photographic chemicals, there are now ranks of computer screens. He would be amazed to watch his images travelling round the world at unimaginable speeds through network and internet lines.

The archive's future is both bright and exciting. Francis Frith, with his unshakeable belief in making photographs available to the greatest number of people, would undoubtedly approve of what is being done today with his lifetime's work. His photographs, depicting our shared past, are now bringing pleasure and enlightenment to millions around the world a century and more after his death.

DARTFORD, HIGH STREET 1902 49017

Dartford is an ancient market-town which grew into a busy industrial centre on the River Darent, at the point where it was crossed by the Roman Watling Street, parts of which lie buried four feet beneath the High Street. The ornate façade of the Bull Hotel with its massive lanterns, on the right, conceals a Georgian galleried yard. Opposite, on the corner of Bullace Lane, is the reputed home of the Kentish rebel leader Wat Tyler.

GRAVESEND, KING STREET 1902 49028

Caddell's Printing Office at number 1, King Street, just visible on the extreme left and next door to the Jackson Brothers' drapery store, was founded by John Samuel Caddell, a stationer, bookbinder, stamp distributor and the publisher of the Gravesend Journal. The entrance to the narrow High Street is just behind the people on the left. The tramcar service, whose tracks are apparent in the foreground, was introduced during the closing decades of the 19th century.

GRAVESEND
Clifton Marine Parade 1902 49042

At Gravesend Reach, the River Thames narrows on its way from the
North Sea to London Bridge, another twenty-six miles upstream. Its
situation, opposite the Essex port of Tilbury, led to its becoming the
pilot station for the Port of London; at the time of this photograph it
was still the world's busiest port. The Thames barges, moored on the
left, and the local bawley boats which trawled for shrimps in the estuary,
were, along with the uninterrupted views of the ships of all nationalities
passing on the river, a source of immense interest for visitors when
Gravesend became a popular resort during the Victorian era.

◆

GRAVESEND, THE ROMAN CATHOLIC CHURCH 1902
49036
Originally built as an Anglican church in Milton Road in 1834, and then purchased for the Catholic community in 1851, St John the Evangelist had its unusual and prominent tower, with a French-style saddleback roof, added to the north-east corner of the building in 1872-3 by Messrs Goldie & Son.

GAD'S HILL PLACE, THE RESIDENCE OF CHARLES DICKENS 1894 34044
This red-brick Georgian house, with bay windows and surmounted by a small white cupola, was coveted by the author Charles Dickens ever since he was a boy living at Chatham; he often passed it on long walks with his father. He eventually purchased it in 1856 and lived here until his death in 1870, while working on his uncompleted novel 'The Mystery of Edwin Drood'. It is now a girls' school. Almost opposite is the Sir John Falstaff inn, named after the events in Shakespeare's 'Henry IV', when the corpulent knight and his companions were set upon by 'men in buckram'. Daniel Defoe reported that the vicinity was noted 'for robbers of seamen after they had received their pay at Chatham'.

COBHAM, THE LEATHER BOTTLE 1894 34046

Situated in the village which was the home of the powerful Cobham family, one of the county's most distinguished families from the time of King John to James I, this half-timbered pub is opposite the church. It was the 'clean and commodious ale-house' where the love-lorn Mr Tracy Tupman stayed in Charles Dickens' 'Pickwick Papers'. A nearby stone inscription also recalls that it was close by that Mr Pickwick found his own remarkable 'inscribed stone'.

BROMPTON, THE GORDON MEMORIAL AND THE ROYAL ENGINEERS INSTITUTE 1894 34043

This 1890 bronze statue of General Gordon of Khartoum on camel-back was the work of E Onslow Ford, and commemorates his illustrious career. It was erected five years after the general's death. He had been in command of the Royal Engineers at Gravesend from 1865-71, and was responsible for the construction of the protective forts along the Thames. The adjacent Royal Engineers Museum contains many Gordon relics, including the folding chair he used at Khartoum, and a yellow jacket given to him by the Emperor of China.

ROCHESTER, COLLEGE GATE AND THE CATHEDRAL 1908 59881
At the foot of Boley Hill stands the 15th-century College Gate, one of three surviving entrances to the precincts of the Cathedral, whose modest spire (added to the original tower in 1904) rises behind. Next door, the Gate House Tea Rooms boasts some lovely 16th-century linenfold wooden panelling.

ROCHESTER, THE CATHEDRAL FROM THE VINES 1894 34027
Two young boys, perhaps pupils from the King's School whose upper storeys and decorated chimneys are visible in the middle foreground inside the cathedral grounds, stand beside a table in the Vines. This public park, with its neatly-trimmed shrubs and bushes, occupies the former site of the vineyard of the Benedictine monastery founded in 1082 by Bishop Gundulf.

ROCHESTER, THE CASTLE AND CATHEDRAL FROM STROOD 1894 34030
The old town of Strood, on the west bank of the River Medway, was incorporated into Rochester in 1835. The 125-foot high keep of the Norman Castle and the tower of the Cathedral dominate this view of the crowded anchorage on a bend of the river, en route to its union with the Thames off Garrison point.

Ospringe, Water Lane 1892 31477
This small village, now subsumed into Faversham, was originally the site of a Roman settlement and subsequently of a hospital and pilgrim hostel founded in 1234 by Henry III.

DAVINGTON, THE PRIORY 1892 31478
The pyramid-capped tower of this Norman church stands prominently on a hill, and forms part of Davington Priory, founded in 1153 by Fulco de Newenham. The adjoining building, resembling a gabled manor house, incorporates the original monastic buildings that housed a small Benedictine nunnery.

CHARTHAM, THE GREEN 1903 50353
This village in the valley of the River Stour has, in fact, two greens: a large open space before the church, and behind it, a small triangular green forming the heart of this rural community round which the cottages and old houses cluster. The pub, with its hanging sign, stands at the far end.

CHARTHAM, THE RIVER 1906 53461

Four young children, seated on the bank of the Stour, are mirrored in the tranquil waters, while to their left, another adult resident stoops to fill a bucket. Two other people stand watching close to the bridge carrying the road on to Chartham Hatch.

CHARTHAM, THE PAPER MILLS AND CHARTHAM HATCH 1906 53454

A splendid panoramic view, taken early in the year, of the Stour Valley looking across to the Julliberrie Downs, with the 14th-century tower of Chartham church rising above the trees. The smoking chimney of the paper mill is in the middle foreground, with the cottages of Chartham Hatch just behind. The team of agricultural workers in the field is preparing the ground for early summer crops.

BISHOPSBOURNE, THE VILLAGE 1903 49416

This village comprises little more than this cluster of charming cottages just off Watling Street, but it has associations with two noted authors. The Elizabethan theologian Richard Hooker wrote his monumental 'Laws of Ecclesiastical Polity' during the five years that he was rector here. He is buried in the local church. In 1919, the former Polish merchant seaman Teodor Jozef Konrad Korzeniowski settled here for the last five years of his life. As Joseph Conrad, he was renowned as a master of the English novel, and is buried at Canterbury.

BARHAM, THE VILLAGE AND THE CHURCH 1903 51062

Many of the sturdy, timber-framed cottages in the centre of this lovely village have been reinforced and decorated with brickwork during the 18th century. The late 13th-century church of St John the Baptist, which forms the focal point of the settlement, had its distinctive green copper spire added during the 19th century, as the result of a gift by a member of the Oxenden family.

BARHAM, THE BRIDGE AND THE RIVER 1903 51061

The flint and stone cottage, with its neatly clipped box hedge and the workshop of C Knight, the local builder and contractor, attached to its side, stands beside the footbridge and ford across the upper reaches of the River Stour.

DOVER, THE ESPLANADE 1899 44793

Here we have a magnificent view of the broad sweep of the breezy seafront at Dover, with the castle overshadowing the town from four hundred feet above, and the Roman Pharos clearly visible beside the medieval St Mary's Church.

DOVER, MARINE PARADE 1892 31418

An assortment of small fishing and rowing boats has been hauled safely above the high water mark in this picture of the eastern end of the Marine Parade; the famous white cliffs are visible beyond the castle jetty. The houses along this stretch of the esplanade were all to be destroyed during World War Two, and then replaced by modern flats.

DOVER, THE CASTLE 1890 25704

One of the very finest fortresses in England, Dover Castle dominates the town and harbour below, with the top of the keep standing 465 feet above sea level. This structure, and the surrounding curtain wall, was built by Henry II in the 12th century at a cost of £7000, but the first fortifications were constructed by King Harold in 1064. Further reinforcements and additions were made over succeeding centuries, until it was regarded as impregnable. Some of the walls are eight metres thick, and the chalk cliff below is honeycombed with passages excavated by invading French troops in the 13th century.

CHARING

High Street 1901 47576

One of Kent's oldest townships, Charing was taken from
Canterbury by the King of Mercia in 757 and assigned
to some of his favourites. It prospered in medieval
times as an important halt for pilgrims on their way to
Canterbury, since it lies just off the North Downs Way.
Henry VIII stayed at the Archbishop's Palace (the manor
house) on his way to the Field of the Cloth of Gold.

CHARING, HIGH STREET 1901 47577

These two views of the steep high street as it winds up the hill towards Canterbury show some of the rich assortment of buildings built of brick or black-and-white half timbering. At the junction of the road leading to Lenham is the grander Pierce House, set back from the road.

CHILHAM, THE SQUARE 1903 50340

Here we see the heart of what many claim is Kent's prettiest village: the tower of its 15th-century flintstone church of St Mary's looks down on this spacious square lined with half-timbered Tudor and Jacobean cottages, houses and shops. The yew tree at the entrance to the churchyard probably pre-dates the building itself. The arrival of modern motor-traffic over subsequent decades means this generous space is now more often used as a crowded car park, and on the Spring Bank Holiday as the setting for an annual Pilgrims' Fayre.

CHILHAM, OLD WIVES' LEES 1908 60355
Lying just to the north of Chilham is this small and curiously named hamlet where, until the beginning of the 20th century, an annual race was staged between two village youths and two maidens for a prize endowed by Sir Dudley Digges, the Master of the Rolls in the early 17th century. His brick Jacobean mansion, Chilham Castle, allegedly designed by Inigo Jones, stands on the west side of the Square at Chilham itself.

GODMERSHAM, THE CHURCH 1906 53453

GODMERSHAM
The Church 1906
Amid scenery loved by the author Jane Austen, who was a frequent visitor here when her brother Edward Knight owned the adjoining 560-acre Godmersham Park, the River Stour flows quietly past the churchyard and its aged yew trees. One is hollow, with sufficient room inside to seat six people. The church, whose Norman tower stands on the north side of the building, has an eastern apse constructed through it, indicating that it was used as a separate chapel.

◆

OLANTIGH
Olantigh Towers 1901
Beside the waters of the Great Stour, this great house in its pleasant parkland marks the original birthplace in 1380 of Cardinal Kempe, the ecclesiastical statesman. He was close to both Henry V and Henry VI, and was responsible for the building of many fine churches; he also suppressed Jack Cade's Kentish rebellion after his appointment as Chancellor in 1450. This substantial mansion, with its impressive portico, has been rebuilt, and is one of three great houses along this stretch of the river.

OLANTIGH, OLANTIGH TOWERS 1901 47557

WYE, BRIDGE STREET 1903 50336

WYE, *Bridge Street 1903*
The half-timbered cottages and the church opposite were originally the site of a priest's seminary founded by Cardinal Kempe. During the 18th century it became a boys' grammar school, and in 1892, the home of Wye Agricultural College.

◆

KENNINGTON
The Mill 1901
Now absorbed into the expanding suburbs of Ashford to the south, this small village once boasted its own imposing windmill on the banks of the Great Stour.

KENNINGTON, THE MILL 1901 47543

HOTHFIELD, THE CHURCH 1901 47549

Hothfield Place was the seat of the Tufton family, but was pulled down after the Second World War. In the 16th century Sir John Tufton entertained Queen Elizabeth I over two days. The 13th-century church of St Margaret, on the edge of the park, was struck by lightning in 1598 and largely burned to the ground. Sir John rebuilt it before his death in 1624, at the age of eighty, and his magnificent tomb is inside, although the bodies of Sir John and his wife were later transferred to Rainham because of water penetration into the family vault below.

PLUCKLEY, THE VILLAGE 1901 47566

On a steep hillside commanding views of the Weald, north-west of Ashford, this charming village was near the seat of the Dering family at the now-vanished Surrenden Dering a mile away. The black horse insignia of the family is displayed on the inn sign of the Dering Arms.

PLUCKLEY, THE VILLAGE 1901 47567
The 19th-century squire, Sir Edward Cholmeley Dering, had every window in the village altered to have rounded lights under an exterior arch in the belief that this would bring good luck. The family, however, were forced to leave their home after suffering financially as a result of the First World War. Nearly ninety years after this photograph was taken, the village was used as the setting for the popular TV drama series 'The Darling Buds of May'.

GREAT CHART, THE VILLAGE 1908 60339
Three small children play on the long village street leading up the hill to the church, lined with well-kept red-brick and timbered cottages and neat gardens, and with the Swan public house halfway along on the right.

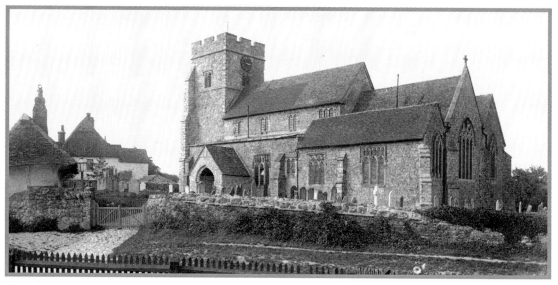

GREAT CHART, THE CHURCH 1901 47552

By the gate leading into the churchyard are the overhanging eaves of the old priest's house, later to become the centre of the local Girl Guides troop. The compact grey stone 14th-century church was rebuilt following a fire in the mid 15th century at the behest of its then rector James Goldwell, who later became the Bishop of Norwich. It contains a number of memorial brasses to six local men who together married a total of fifteen wives; two of them each married no less than five times. They include Captain Nicholas Toke, who set out at the age of ninety-three to walk to London in 1680 to find a sixth bride, but died before encountering her.

ASHFORD, HIGH STREET 1901 47521

The broad High Street, once the site of the market established under a charter from Edward I, was, at the turn of the last century, still very much a rendezvous for the cattle and sheep farmers of the Weald and Romney Marsh.

ASHFORD, HIGH STREET 1901 47522
Several 18th-century stone facades are apparent in these pictures, and some of the other old houses are disguised by contemporary shop fronts. On the extreme left in this photograph the pinnacles of the church's 120-foot Perpendicular central tower can be seen rising above the buildings.

WILLESBOROUGH, THE VILLAGE 1909 61560
East of Ashford, and now subsumed by it, the little village of Willesborough possesses two landmark structures. The originally 13th-century church has undergone substantial rebuilding, and is now graced by this curious 'candle-snuffer' shingled spire, incorporating small windows round it.

WILLESBOROUGH, THE WINDMILL 1909 61562
Willesborough's second landmark is the white-painted windmill, which dominates the opposite end of the village.

NEWINGTON, THE VILLAGE 1903 50392

NEWINGTON
The Village 1903

Just off the road between Lyminge
and Hythe, this jettied timber-frame
cottage stands at the approach to the
13th-century church. The church has a
distinctive wooden belfry topped by a
flattened cupola of lead, all supported
from within by a remarkable structure
of curious timbers. In 1201, the Lord
of Folkestone and the Earl of Guisnes
fought for ownership of the village in
a trial by battle. The Earl won, and
Newington was granted to the Abbey of
Guisnes in Flanders.

◆

BILSINGTON
The Village 1909

A handsome farm cart stands in the yard
of a timber-framed two-storey building,
in this small hamlet on the road between
Tenterden and Hythe. Close by are
the ruined walls of a 13th-century
Augustinian priory founded in 1253 by
Sir John Maunsell, a priest's son who
became a counsellor to Henry III.

BILSINGTON, THE VILLAGE 1909 61578

CHERITON

Ashley Avenue 1908 60387

Now a crowded suburb of Folkestone, this once rural village on the heights of the Downs just behind Sandgate has been transformed by the construction and rail links accompanying the building of the huge Eurotunnel project. These small boys and girls can have had no idea how these quiet roads, with their trim family homes, would have been ravaged within the coming century by the effects of modern development.

FOLKESTONE
The Leas 1901 48052
In the year of Queen Victoria's passing, these
fashionably-clad Edwardians take the air along the
mile-long greensward of The Leas on top of the cliff,
and against the backdrop of these smart Victorian
villas. Charles Dickens had earlier taken similar
constitutional walks along this route while writing the
opening chapters of 'Little Dorrit' in 1855.

FOLKESTONE, SS 'DUCHESS OF YORK' 1897 39560
The foundation of Folkestone's prosperity during the 19th century, these packet boats conveying passengers across the Channel to the coast of France some twenty-six miles away transformed Folkestone from a small fishing village into a major entry and departure port of Britain. After Dover, it is now the busiest of the Channel ports, although these twin-funnelled paddle steamers have long since given way to massive sea-going catamarans.

FOLKESTONE, THE HARVEY STATUE 1887 19963

A hooded bathchair stands before the Victorian buildings and the bronze statue of William Harvey, a 16th-century native of the town; he achieved renown for his work in discovering the fact that blood circulates within the body through the network of arteries, veins and capillaries. He holds a heart in his hand. In the company of the young sons of Charles I, he watched the Battle of Edgehill during the English Civil War, before dying in 1657 after reputedly taking poison after learning that he was losing his sight.

FOLKESTONE, CLIFTON ROAD 1890 25886

The coming of the railway to the town in 1843 not only sparked the massive increase in people arriving from London, seventy-one miles away, en route for the Continent, but also Folkestone's growth as a fashionable resort. These stately Victorian houses were part of the huge process of building development that ensued. In the distance is the Palace Theatre, now re-christened the Leas Pavilion.

SANDGATE

High Street 1906 56952

The weatherboarded cottages are prominent among the stone fronted shops and restaurants, whose rich assortment of goods and services are lavishly advertised. The elegant lamp posts were a relatively new addition to this picturesque commercial setting, and although the rails carrying the tramcars are evident, it is clear that pedal-power and horse-drawn transport had yet to be displaced by the internal combustion engine.

SANDGATE, THE PARADE 1899 44774

Westwards from Folkestone, and now linked to it as a suburb, Sandgate shared in the popularity of its neighbour as a seaside resort around the turn of the century. Near the cliffs in the distance are the remains of the castle built by Henry VIII in 1539 as part of his coastal defensive scheme; it is one of the four he constructed in Kent. This building was augmented in 1806 during the threat of a Napoleonic invasion.

SANDGATE, HIGH STREET 1903 50370

It is mid-afternoon in the quiet main street of Sandgate, with a single-decker tramcar passing by on its way to Folkestone. On the hill beyond stands a Martello tower and the fortifications of Shorncliffe Camp, whose construction was undertaken under Sir John Moore during the Napoleonic War. His work is commemorated in a memorial near the seashore, on the site of a house where he lived.

SALTWOOD, THE CASTLE 1902 48830

Built in 1154 by Henry de Essex on the edge of a valley, this high-walled building became the residence of the Archbishops of Canterbury. Here, in 1170, and in darkness, four knights met with Randolph de Broc, the then tenant, to plan the murder of Thomas Becket, and set out the next day from here to accomplish their mission. The keep was restored as a country mansion in 1882, and subsequently became the home of art historian Sir Kenneth Clark and his son and heir, the Conservative politician Alan Clark.

SALTWOOD, THE VILLAGE 1902 48831
Like so many little Kent villages, with its cottages and houses clustered around a small green, Saltwood epitomises the rural atmosphere of the county at the turn of the last century.

SALTWOOD, THE VILLAGE HALL AND THE ALMSHOUSES 1902 48832
The half-timbered village hall, with its adjacent rows of almshouses, overlooks this peaceful scene with its curiously maternal architecture.

HYTHE, HIGH STREET 1899 44785
The long, narrow High Street, with the Rose & Crown Inn on the right, is at the foot of a steep hill overlooking the sea. In the distance is the Town Hall of 1794, with its colonnaded portico and its clock jutting out over the carriageway.

HYTHE, THE CRICKET GROUND 1899 44788
Surrounded by these majestic trees, and with the west tower of St Leonard's Church, one of the largest and finest in Kent, rising behind them, a summer game of cricket takes place on this spacious ground; the bowler embarks on his run up to the wicket as the batsman and fielders await his arrival at the crease.

HYTHE
The School of Musketry 1903 50380
Standing in Military Road, north-west of Red Lion
Square, is the School of Small Arms, the main school
of army musketry, founded here in 1854. Its training
ranges are situated on the desolate shingle
banks west of the town.

CANTERBURY, THE CATHEDRAL c1875 12053

CANTERBURY
The Cathedral c1875

Soaring above the surrounding rooftops, the spires of the Cathedral dominate the city in this view taken from the tower of the West Gate. St Peter's Street and the High Street wind into the distance on the right, with the smaller towers of St Peter's church and St George's church visible just off to the left of the thoroughfare.

CANTERBURY
The Cathedral 1888

A springtime photograph of the massive and imposing cathedral, the first in Britain and the seat of the Primate of All England, as well as one of Europe's most celebrated places of pilgrimage. It was begun in 1070 by Archbishop Lanfranc, with the central Bell Harry tower being completed in 1500 and the north-west tower added between 1831 and 1840; this picture gives an excellent impression of the grandeur of the 188-foot long nave, which soars to a vault eighty feet above.

CANTERBURY, THE CATHEDRAL 1888 21357

CANTERBURY, ST JOHN'S HOSPITAL GATEWAY 1898 40848
Here we see the half-timbered gatehouse of the Hospital of St John, founded by Archbishop Lanfranc in 1084 and the second oldest medieval almshouse in England, which stands in Northgate Street, outside the original city walls close to the River Stour.

PATRIXBOURNE, THE VILLAGE 1903 49411

The late Norman church, with its tower surmounted by a 13th-century shingled spire, was built around 1160 and stands in its small churchyard shaded by a selection of conifer trees. The Tudor-style houses in the village are, however, imitations constructed around the middle of the 19th century.

LITTLEBOURNE, THE VILLAGE 1903 49427

Littlebourne is one of the charming little villages in the heart of the orchard country which stretches between Canterbury and Wingham; its cottages present an unusual mixture of architectural styles. On the left-hand side of the street, the ventilators of the oast house project from the roof.

ICKHAM, THE CHURCH 1903 49434

This fine Early English church, set back from the village and behind a narrow green, boasts a raised 13th-century chancel and a tapering, shingled broach spire. Behind the barn is the red-brick rectory where the great 17th-century scholar Meric Casaubon lived and died. He is buried in Canterbury Cathedral.

WICKHAMBREAUX, THE POST OFFICE 1903 51048

On the banks of the Little Stour, whose waters flow peacefully under the bridge on the left, the small general stores and post office on the right served this little hidden village with its 18th- and 19th-century brick cottages.

WICKHAMBREAUX, THE FORGE 1903 49425

FORDWICH, FROM THE BRIDGE 1899 44228

WICKHAMBREAUX
The Forge 1903
At a time when farming still depended on natural horsepower, rather than the mechanical variety, the local forge was an integral part of any local community. This long, low building, with its shingled roof and solid square chimney above the forge itself, is adorned with tattered auction flyers.

◆

FORDWICH
From the Bridge 1899
A town when the Domesday Book was compiled, and a settled place as far back as the 7th century, Fordwich was a flourishing port on the River Stour for Canterbury when the river was still navigable. The thousands of tons of Caen stone for the building of the cathedral were landed here. The twelve rooms of the riverside George and Dragon still offer accommodation.

STURRY, THE CHURCH 1899 44223

The 15th-century tower of the church stands on Norman foundations, and houses the tomb of the last abbot of St Augustine's abbey at Canterbury who, at the time of the Dissolution, was given the manor of Sturry. He survived only another two years. The red-brick gateway on the left leads to the garden of Milner Court, the home of the statesman Lord Milner, which is now the Junior King's School of Canterbury.

HERNE BAY, THE GARDENS 1897 40156

Two enterprising businessmen laid out this seaside resort in the early 1830s, and the arrival of the railway in 1833 encouraged its growth. By the time this picture was taken, it had become a highly fashionable watering-place to stay in the summer months. On the extreme right, the three-quarter mile pier can be glimpsed.

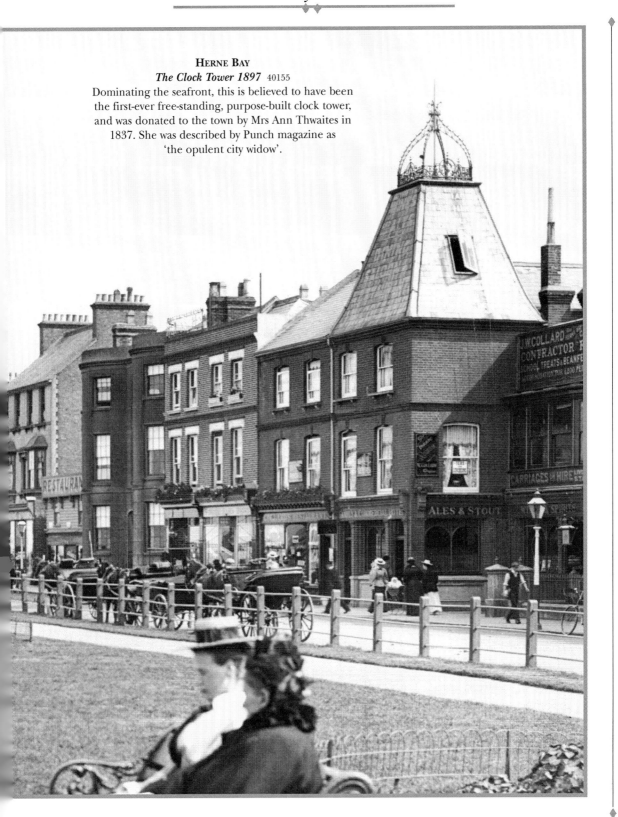

HERNE BAY
The Clock Tower 1897 40155
Dominating the seafront, this is believed to have been the first-ever free-standing, purpose-built clock tower, and was donated to the town by Mrs Ann Thwaites in 1837. She was described by Punch magazine as 'the opulent city widow'.

HERNE BAY, FROM THE PIER 1897 40152

The pier, the second longest in the country after Southend's, reached out from the mile and a half long esplanade and was built in 1832 to shorten the time taken to travel to the continent. Boats travelling down the Thames estuary from London were met by stagecoaches here, and their passengers were transported onward by road to Dover. The Grand Pier Pavilion was opened by the Lord Mayor of London in 1910, but was gutted by fire in 1970.

MARGATE, THE HARBOUR 1906 54762

This was the home of the local fishing fleet, many of whose vessels are seen moored here at low tide. During the reign of Elizabeth I this little port also maintained about twenty small sailing boats, locally called 'hoys', which carried passengers along the coast and on the Thames. From this came the nautical cry of 'ahoy'. They continued to operate into the 19th century, until ousted by the steam packet service in about 1815.

MARGATE
Marine Parade 1908 60359

Benjamin Beale, a local glovemaker and a Quaker, invented the bathing machine in 1751 to conserve ladies' modesty while they took a dip in the briny. These cumbersome devices were backed into the sea by horses, and the incumbent then disembarked down steps at the rear, protected from cold winds and inquisitive stares by a collapsible umbrella attached to the back of the vehicle. Their introduction sparked the transformation of Margate from a fishing village into the most popular resort in Kent; a process which was further encouraged by the arrival of the railway, which offered speedy and inexpensive travel from London. This view is looking across a crowded beach towards the harbour, the stone pier and the lighthouse.

MARGATE
The Sands 1906 54758

Young day-trippers on the beach are preparing to enjoy a traditional ride on one of the
six donkeys retained here for the purpose during the summer months. The weather-
beaten, tanned faces of their two handlers bear testimony to the resort's sunshine record.
The spectators on the thronged promenade and beach behind are apparently watching
a pierrot show being staged in a flimsy wooden theatre. The Cinque Ports Arms is a
reflection of the fact that Margate was a member of the Cinque Ports attached to Dover.

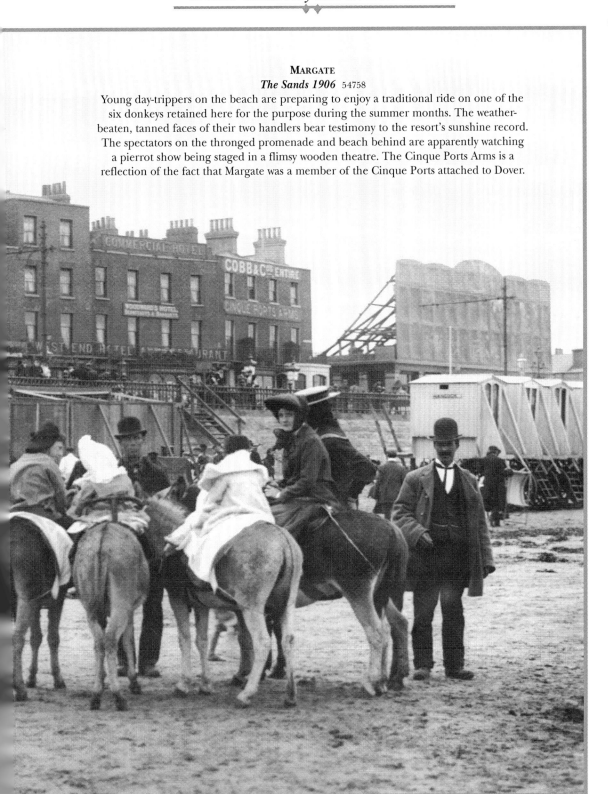

RECULVER
The Beach and the Towers 1892 31456

The famous twin towers of the Norman church, built on the site
of an earlier Saxon abbey and the centre of the Roman fortress
of Regulbium, built around AD 280 by Carausius, were for many
centuries a landmark for shipping in the Thames, and stand
at the northern end of the Wantsum channel. But erosion of
the coastline prompted the demolition with gunpowder of the
church in 1809; the towers, known as the Two Sisters, were sold
to Trinity House, who restored them as a navigational aid. The
foundations of the fortress can be traced around the site from
the King Ethelbert Inn.

WESTGATE ON SEA
The Hotels and the Beach 1890 27463
While the neighbouring resort of Margate had been attracting
hordes of trippers from London from 1753 onwards, Westgate
remained a more sedate and favoured place for families
throughout the late Victorian and Edwardian era, with its broad
sandy beaches and red-brick hotels. Its atmosphere is exemplified
in this photograph showing families genteelly disporting
themselves on the beach in front of St Mildred's Hotel and Bathing
Establishment; one can only speculate at the discomfort these
ladies and children must have endured in the summer heat in their
voluminous clothing, even with a cooling onshore breeze.

DUMPTON GAP 1894 34194
To the east of Margate, and south of Foreness Point, Kingsgate Bay is marked by this gap in the cliffs. It was originally called Bartholomew's Gate, but was changed by order of Charles II who landed here in 1683, accompanied by the Duke of York, on his way to London.

BROADSTAIRS, THE SANDS 1887 19707
The 'rare good sands', as Charles Dickens described them, still form the focal point of this 'old-fashioned watering place' where 'Nicholas Nickleby', 'David Copperfield', 'The Old Curiosity Shop', and 'Barnaby Rudge' were all written by him in houses overlooking this same view. A fishing hamlet in 1837 when he first visited, it quickly expanded into the quiet family resort it remains today.

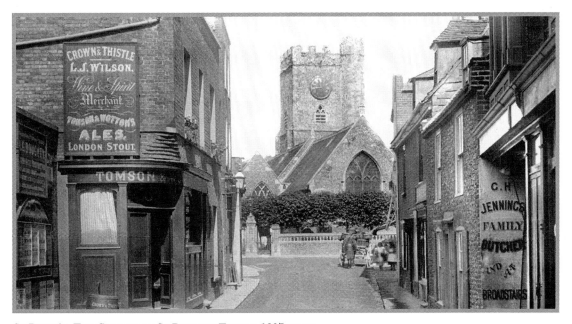

ST PETER'S, THE CHURCH OF ST-PETER-IN-THANET 1897 39587
Originally a separate village from Broadstairs and taking its name from the medieval church, this small collection of shops and houses lies inland from the sea. The great, grey battlemented tower stands eighty-two feet high and was used as a signalling station, continuously manned by four men, during the Napoleonic war. As a result it was afforded the rare privilege of flying the White Ensign.

BROADSTAIRS, YORK GATE 1887 19726
Leading from the old village to the harbour beyond, this 16th-century arch, originally fitted with a portcullis and gates, was built to protect the settlement against pirates and smugglers. It narrowly escaped demolition in the early part of the 19th century.

BROADSTAIRS, THE HARBOUR 1897 39591
Rows of bathing machines along the shoreline and in front of the low white cliffs demonstrate the popularity, and prevailing prudery, of immersion in sea-water among the Victorian visitors. The shallow-draught Thames sailing barge aground on the sands dominates this photograph, taken from the foot of the Elizabethan stone jetty. The cumbersome leeboards, which helped the vessel to maintain a course, are clearly visible amidships.

BROADSTAIRS, THE BEACH 1907 58325
The wheeled bathing machines of earlier pictures have been replaced by this array of circular tents, allowing Edwardians to divest themselves in privacy. Although changes in fashion meant that clothing was no longer as restrictive and cumbersome as that of the previous century, changing for a swim must still have been a prolonged and intricate affair. The line of new hotels along the cliff-top, including the white stuccoed Albion Hotel, and the crowded beach, are a clear indication of the resort's appeal to holidaymakers.

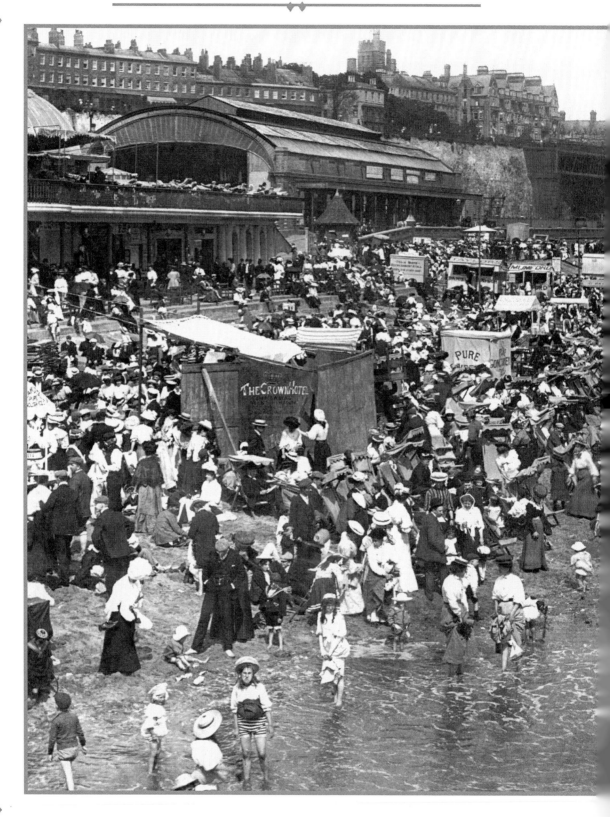

RAMSGATE

The Beach 1907 58272

The sandy beach is overwhelmed by a tide of holidaymakers, most of whom have probably arrived here by train at the station in the left background. This was the terminus of the London, Chatham and Dover Railway and had opened in October 1863. It was closed in 1926, and Ramsgate Station moved to the rear of the town. In the background is the Promenade Pier, built in 1881.

RAMSGATE, VICTORIA PARADE 1901 48039

Ramsgate is the third in the trinity of Thanet holiday resorts; its attractions would have been familiar to the young
Princess Victoria, who as a small girl stayed in a house near the bandstand on the left of the picture, and played
freely on the sands below. As Queen Empress, she died in the year this picture was taken. The Saint Cloud Hotel
and the Granville Hotel, whose impressive colonnaded and balconied frontages face the sea, catered for the
middle classes and their families.

RAMSGATE, THE ROYAL PAVILION 1906 53466

Opened in June 1904, this elegant structure, sited at one end of the harbour, was designed to cater for pleasure-
seekers in all kinds of weather. The upper deck offered the opportunity for a 300-yard stroll around the outside
of the main auditorium, while listening to a brass band. Inside, the capacious great hall, 130 feet long by 65 feet,
offered a range of other entertainments and was used for plays and concerts. After 1911, a skating rink was added
to the facilities. Beneath the building holidaymakers could seek shelter from inclement weather. Beyond the
pavilion, the arms of the east and west piers encircling the harbour can be seen, with the latter's lighthouse just
visible on the right.

PEGWELL BAY, THE COASTGUARD COTTAGES 1907 58306
This row of diminutive, white cottages provided accommodation for the Coastguards maintaining a watch along this busy stretch of the Kent coastline with its treacherous offshore sandbanks. The bay, with its wide sandy beach, was almost certainly the landing place of the Danish brothers Hengist and Horsa, who came to Britain in 449AD to fight for the British king Vortigern against the marauding Picts.

SANDWICH, THE BARBICAN AND THE BRIDGE 1894 34212
Originally the first of the Cinque Ports, its Saxon harbour had silted up by the late 14th century, ending its role as the chief place of embarkation for the Continent and as England's premier naval station. On the right, carrying the road from Ramsgate, is the swing bridge over the River Stour of 1863, which replaced the original drawbridge of 1757. On the far side is the Bridgegate, usually called the Barbican, built in 1539 with semi-circular flanking bastions, and which is one of a chain of similar blockhouses constructed during the reign of Henry VIII.

DEAL
From the Pier 1899 44204
Somewhere along this steeply-sloping, shingle beach the armoured
legionaries from Julius Caesar's invading army waded ashore in 55BC.
In the days when sail reigned supreme, this was once the main harbour
town in south-east England, servicing ships moored in the shallow waters
of the Downs, between the treacherous Goodwin Sands and the shore.
In the centre of this picture is the Time Ball Tower, used for supplying
the correct time to the anchored vessels. Originally built as a semaphore
station at the end of the 18th century, relaying messages from the
Downs to London in two minutes, the time ball was added in 1855.
A replica of the one at the Greenwich Observatory, and electrically
connected to it, the dark ball started to rise up its mast at 12.55, and was
dropped at exactly 1 pm.

DEAL, THE ESPLANADE 1899 44207

DEAL
The Esplanade 1899

The Beach House Temperance Hotel (to the right in photograph No 44204) is apparent on the left in this view of the broad Esplanade, looking towards the centre of the town. The straw boaters and caps worn by all the males reflect the prevailing etiquette and fashion of the time. On the extreme right is one of the winches used by local fishermen to haul their boats up the shingle beach above the high water mark, since Deal had no harbour of its own.

◆

ST MARGARET'S AT CLIFFE
The Village 1898

This little village stands on the edge of a cove in the chalk cliffs of South Foreland, where the road drops steeply down to St Margaret's Bay; it clusters around an impressive Norman church, built around 1150-60, whose gateway is just on the extreme left of the picture. A team of plough horses wait quietly in the village street outside the Carrier's Arms.

ST MARGARET'S AT CLIFFE, THE VILLAGE 1898 40816

**ST MARGARET'S BAY,
THE SOUTH FORELAND LOWER LIGHT 1898** 40814

ST MARGARET'S BAY
The South Foreland Lower Light 1898

Three hundred feet above the sea, this white-painted Victorian lighthouse housed a two-ton turntable operating the revolving light. It was built in 1843; for a further ninety years after this photograph was taken, it offered both a warning and guidance for ships passing north along the white cliffs, and for those heading for Dover harbour to the south, to avoid the Goodwin Sands.

◆

ST MARGARET'S BAY
'Excelsior' 1903

These timber-clad cottages, standing at the foot of the white cliffs, are part of a small community which developed both as a bathing resort and as a residential quarter in the closing years of the 19th century. The adjoining sandy beach has been the starting point for generations of Channel swimmers since the days of Captain Matthew Webb's successful feat in 1875. The popular composer Noel Coward later owned one of the small houses here.

ST MARGARET'S BAY, 'EXCELSIOR' 1903 50404

EYNSFORD, THE VILLAGE 1905 53257

This picture postcard village is strung out along the road, with the River Darent running through it and under the 15th-century humpbacked bridge (seen here behind the horse and cart) alongside a ford; it possesses an assortment of Tudor brick and timbered cottages. The church of St Martin was originally Norman; its spindly 13th-century wood-shingled spire is augmented by a brightly-painted clock-face, which was added the year before this photograph was taken.

EYNSFORD, THE VILLAGE STREET 1905 53251

The gateway on the right, facing the Eynsford Castle Inn, leads to the ruins of the Norman castle which was the property of William of Eynsford. In 1163 he became involved in a dispute with Archbishop Thomas Becket over the appointment of a local priest. Henry II supported William in his case, but after Becket's martyrdom at Canterbury, he was so filled with remorse that he left the castle and entered a monastery.

OTFORD, THE ARCHBISHOP'S PALACE 1895 36418

Built by Archbishop Warham in the early 16th century, this small manor house, consisting of a three-storey brick tower, a gallery (later turned into cottages), and the single-storey storehouse beyond, was 'given' by Cranmer to Henry VIII. He, in turn, made it into a residence for Princess Mary. During the reign of Edward VI, the lead was stripped from the roof and the building descended into decay. The palace's water supply was allegedly started by Thomas Becket who, dissatisfied with the purity of local water, tapped his crozier on the ground and two springs bubbled forth.

WROTHAM, HIGH STREET 1901 47636

The narrow high street leading to a small square boasted a varied selection of businesses at the turn of the last century. On the right hand side is Wagland's bakery, with the Wrotham Cycle Works and its hanging sign a few doors along towards the George & Dragon Inn. On the left-hand corner of the street, J Coleman's operation combined the service of local undertaker with that of grocer and draper.

WROTHAM, THE VILLAGE 1904 52831

The 13th-century church with its 15th-century tower stands on the north side of the square. At the foot of the tower, a vaulted passageway extends right through it, enabling processions to take place around the west end of the church without leaving consecrated ground. This would otherwise have been impossible, since the adjoining highway abuts the building. Inside this feature is a stone that may have once held a sanctuary ring, which granted safety to any alleged criminals who grasped it.

IGHTHAM, THE VILLAGE 1901 47624

This delightful rambling village acquired its name from the Saxon king Ehta, or Otha's settlement. But nearby Oldbury Hill has traces of Neanderthal hunters and an Iron Age fort on its slopes. For many years the village shop here in Ightham was kept by Benjamin Harrison, who achieved international recognition in the Victorian era for his archaeological work in this area. He died in 1921 at the age of eighty-four, and is commemorated in a tablet in the local church.

SEVENOAKS, THE CONSTITUTIONAL CLUB 1895 36399

The foundation stone of this building was laid with two gold sovereigns beneath it, not in the north-east corner but at the southern end of the building, in 1889. Standing between the Dartford Road and Seal Hollow, and with its Club Hall visible on the north side, it was built by the Constitutional Club company for social and political meetings, and contained billiards, smoking and committee rooms, refreshment bar and cloakrooms. It was later adapted as offices for a firm of local solicitors.

SEVENOAKS,
The Vine Cricket Ground 1895 36407
One suspects that these groups of children, with one accompanying nursemaid, seated on the benches and the steps of the canopied bandstand, have been induced to pose by the photographer, to complement this carefully-composed photograph. The houses beyond stood in the Dartford Road. The ground was given to the town in perpetuity in the late 18th century by the 3rd Duke of Dorset. It is possibly the oldest cricket ground in England, with the first fully reported match between Kent and Sussex taking place here on 9 September 1734.

IVY HATCH, THE VILLAGE 1901 47617

IVY HATCH
The Village 1901
This tiny, attractive hamlet close to the great manor house of Ightham Mote has one small shop, the Plough Inn selling beers brewed at Westerham near the county border, and several ivy-clad cottages.

PLAXTOL
Dunk's Green 1901
Some fine stone and brick cottages and an oast house stand along the road leading towards Mereworth Woods near the village centre of Plaxtol, on the edge of the Ragstone Ridge. This is a strangely remote part of the county, whose beauty is guarded and reserved, although surrounded by the richness of the Weald.

PLAXTOL, DUNK'S GREEN 1901 47611

TONBRIDGE

High Street 1890 T1015004

The late 15th-century half-timbered Chequers Inn, with its gabled
frontage and a swinging sign said to have been put up in the
reign of Elizabeth I, stands on the west side of this busy street.
Next door is a fine town house, now a restaurant, but which
at the time of this photograph was occupied by a pawnbroker,
whose sign of three gold balls can be seen on the upper storey.
Further along on the opposite side of the street is the Rose and
Crown, a 16th-century building which was altered two hundred
years later by being given a chequered brick front. Above the
porch are the arms of the Duchess of Kent, Queen Victoria's
mother, who stayed here before her daughter's accession.

TONBRIDGE, HIGH STREET 1890 T1015001

Another view of the High Street at a less congested point and on a very hot and sunny summer's day: the shopkeepers have lowered their sun-blinds to protect their wares, and the lady on the left has unfurled her parasol. The London to Hastings road passed through this section of the town, and with the coming of motor vehicles this street became a traffic bottleneck.

TONBRIDGE, HOP WASHING 1890 T1015009

A team of farm-workers undertakes the laborious task of spraying a field of hops with liquid soap, or possibly a copper solution, to ward off insects and fungal disease as the crop nears harvesting. The process, using hand pumps attached to the horse-drawn reservoirs, was not very efficient. It was interspersed with dusting the growing vines with sulphur and nicotine compounds, but was essential. It was not unknown for entire crops to be laid waste if this work was not undertaken at regular intervals during the growing season.

TONBRIDGE, BARDEN PARK, THE AVENUE 1890 T1015003

The manor of Barden lay to the south-west of Tonbridge. Barden Park House and its estate was in the possession of the Abrey family during the latter part of the 19th century. During the First World War the house was occupied by the military authorities, and was used for the confinement of captured German officer prisoners. At the conclusion of hostilities, the house and estate was purchased by Tonbridge Urban District Council and was used to build one of the first council estates.

CHIDDINGSTONE, THE CHURCH 1891 29400

The fine 14th-century church of St Mary, built of local sandstone, has a Perpendicular tower with dumpy crocketed pinnacles and full-length aisles of the same width as the nave and chancel. It was extensively rebuilt and restored by Sir Bartholomew Burghersh after a lightning strike and fire in 1624, when its Jacobean porch, pulpit and font were added. The latter, with its unusual cover, cost £3. 10s.

CHIDDINGSTONE, THE VILLAGE 1891 29398

This unspoiled row of 16th- and 17th-century half-timbered houses facing onto the church was built and owned mainly by small farmers and tradesmen, who formed the backbone of the rural affluent society. Behind the houses is the 'Chiding Stone', a bulbous lump of sandstone to which scolds were brought to learn the error of their ways; legend has it that it gave the village its name, but it is more likely to have been derived from 'Ciddingas', the people of a Saxon named Cidd.

HEVER, CHIPPENS BANK ROAD 1906 53556
Three children, who have possibly been out gathering some of the autumnal hedgerow harvest in this bountiful part of the country, stand at one side of the sunken lane. Its steep banks and overhanging trees would have provided protection for travellers when the winter storms came.

HEVER, THE VILLAGE 1906 53548

Hever is intimately associated with Anne Boleyn, who spent her childhood here in the company of her father Sir Thomas Bullen, the Earl of Wiltshire, whose tomb is at the little church of St Peter. Its slim spire, set against a backdrop of trees, rises above the broad plain of the River Eden, and is visible for several miles away.

EDENBRIDGE, HIGH STREET 1906 54271

This main street was once part of the Roman road which ran from London to Lewes in West Sussex. The legionaries paved it with ragstone eighteen feet wide and seven inches thick. The Crown Inn, whose signboard hangs above the carriageway, was built in the 15th century by Sir William Taylor, the Lord Mayor of London in 1469.

PENSHURST, THE VILLAGE 1891 29386

The charming village of Penshurst lies in a valley at the junction of the River Eden and the Medway; it is renowned for the stately mansion of Penshurst Place, the home of the Sidney family since the reign of Edward VI. The church of St John the Baptist, originally built between the 13th and 15th centuries, has a late Perpendicular tower, glimpsed through the trees here, and its interior, largely remodelled by Sir Gilbert Scott in 1864-5, contains a number of the Sidney family tombs and memorials.

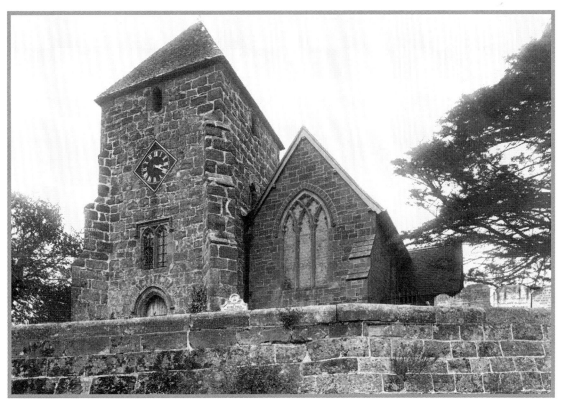

BIDBOROUGH, THE CHURCH 1896 37903

The church of St Lawrence is superbly positioned on the brow of a narrow spur offering splendid views to the north of the Greensand Hills. Built of sandstone and dating back to Saxon times, although with a Norman nave and chancel, it still has a number of small pews for children installed in 1790 at the beginning of the Sunday School movement.

SOUTHBOROUGH, THE PARADE 1896 37890
Since it was gradually absorbed to become a suburb of Royal Tunbridge Wells, this small village south of Tonbridge supported a number of businesses in its commercial centre. Apart from G P Mansell's valuation and estate agency operation seen in the centre of the picture, F Simmons's tailoring concern offered liveries for wealthy households with domestic staff, and cycle suits, reflecting the growing popularity of this pursuit at the turn of the century.

SOUTHBOROUGH, LONDON ROAD 1900 44920
This is the same scene as photograph No 37890 in the opposite direction, four years later, revealing the rich assortment of buildings and businesses which had developed along this stretch of the main highway running between London and the seaside resort of Eastbourne. On the left-hand side, W Cushen, a silk mercer and undertaker's office, is followed by a fruiterer and greengrocer's, a stationery shop, a barber's, and a fishmonger. On the near side of the road, a farm cart carries a churn of milk.

SOUTHBOROUGH, HOLDEN CORNER 1896 37896
The sloping common, with its tranquil pond and surrounding trees, has attracted one straw-boatered angler. On the extreme left, in Holden Road, is the substantial two-and-a-half storied Holder House, built of red brick around 1800 with a Doric-columned porch.

ROYAL TUNBRIDGE WELLS, MOUNT EPHRAIM 1885 T87004
Viewed from the common, Mount Ephraim was given its name by the Dissenters. By the end of the 17th century it had been rapidly developed by the building of shops, taverns, hotels and houses as the town flourished as a fashionable spa resort.

ROYAL TUNBRIDGE WELLS, THE PANTILES 1890 T87001
Nearly four hundred feet above sea level, this principal inland resort of Kent owes its popularity to the accidental discovery of a chalybeate spring by Dudley, Lord North in 1606, which led to the fashion, amongst the nobility, to visit and take the waters. The terraced walk of the Pantiles, with its row of shops behind a colonnade faced by lime trees, was first laid out in 1638. It received its name from the tiles with a concave surface with which it was paved in 1697 at the instigation of Princess (later Queen) Anne.

AYLESFORD, PRESTON HALL AND THE FOUNTAIN 1898 41554

AYLESFORD
Preston Hall and the Fountain 1898
Preston Hall was built for the businessman and entrepreneur Edward Ladd Betts by the architect John Thomas in the Jacobean style in 1850. The fountain, also by Thomas, was added the following year. The mansion was described by Pevsner as one which 'could hardly be drearier'. Within fifty years of this photograph it had become a chest hospital.

◆

BEARSTED
The Church 1898
The 15th-century Perpendicular west tower of the Church of the Holy Cross is remarkable for the three sculptures of heraldic lions, which crouch at the corners of the battlements. They are replacements for those which were originally in place; the exposed position caused weathering, which was already very noticeable during the lifetime of the 17th-century Kentish historian Edward Hasted.

BEARSTED, THE CHURCH 1898 41566

MAIDSTONE, ALLINGTON CASTLE 1898 41547

This romantic-looking castle, set in a bend of the River Medway, was founded in early Norman times, and rebuilt in the late 13th century by Sir Stephen de Penchester, the Warden of the Cinque Ports. Further alterations were made by the Wyatt family when it came into their possession in 1493, and Sir Thomas Wyatt, the father of the English sonnet, was born here in 1503. The buildings were to undergo further extensive restoration at the hands of the mountaineer Lord Martin Conway eight years after this picture was taken.

MAIDSTONE, ALLINGTON LOCKS 1898 41548

The River Medway broadens at Maidstone, on its way to meet the Thames estuary, and the locks here were built in 1792 and mark the tidal limit of the waterway. Along this stretch of the river, the tan-sailed barges carrying cargoes of paper and timber, and the 'stumpies', or narrow boats, used to convey bricks from the kilns down river, were once a familiar sight.

LOOSE, THE VILLAGE 1898 41560

Two miles south of Maidstone, this little secretive village perched on a hillside once had thirteen watermills within its boundaries, powered by the two main streams flowing into the River Medway. The shingle spire of All Saints Church rises above the surrounding houses, while halfway up the hill is the Tudor timbered Old Wool House, in which the fleeces of sheep were washed.

HEADCORN, THE VILLAGE 1903 51065

During the 15th century, Headcorn was a cloth-making centre which prospered with the arrival of Flemish weavers, and its single, long street has several fine buildings dating back to that time. The Perpendicular church of St Peter and Paul dates back in part to the 13th century, and the upper part of its porch was once used as a prison. On the south side of the street are several half-timbered houses of notable quality, with Shakespeare House and its prominent gable, and the Chequers Inn, both very evident.

Leeds Castle 1892 31498

Originally a wooden Saxon fortress built on two islands in a natural moat formed by the river Len, it was transformed into a solid stone castle at the beginning of the 12th century by the Norman baron Robert de Crevecoeur. For three centuries it was the dower home of eight medieval queens in succession. Much loved by Henry VIII, who lavished substantial sums on its improvement, it was then owned in turn by the St Leger, Culpeper and Fairfax families, who all played major roles in settling the colonies of the New World. The south front was recast in 1822.

STAPLEHURST, THE VILLAGE 1903 51070

This long and irregular village stands on either side of a switchback rise in the otherwise dead-straight Roman road that comprises this section of the A229. The curious raised pavements on either side of the street are possibly a development designed to counteract the effects of heavy rain. The 15th-century tower of All Saints church rises in the background; its famous carved wooden southern door from the 12th century, showing an assortment of Viking motifs, still attracts visitors.

HORSMONDEN, THE GREEN 1903 50552

The village of half-timbered and weatherboarded buildings clusters around the green, known locally as 'the Heath', but the village church itself is nearly two miles away.

HORSMONDEN, THE GREEN 1903 50553
The settlement was once the centre of a local iron-working industry, and the white-painted Gun Inn with its swinging signboard was where John Browne, the local ironmaster, designed ordnance for the navies of both sides in the 17th-century Anglo-Dutch wars.

GOUDHURST

The Village Church 1901 46378

This high village of the Weald looks out on a panoramic view of orchards and hopfields, although the foundation of its prosperity in the Middle Ages was based on weaving and iron-working. When these declined in the 18th century, they were replaced by smuggling. On the right is the half-timbered frontage of The Star and Eagle Inn, which was a centre for this nefarious trade and is connected to the church by a secret underground passage. The large squat tower of St Mary's was built between 1638-40 at a cost of £750. In 1747, the Goudhurst Militia fought a fierce battle with the Hawkhurst gang of smugglers in the churchyard, while the villagers sought sanctuary within the building's sandstone walls. In the basement of the house on the left of the picture, William Rootes had a bicycle repair shop, the forerunner of the Rootes Motor Group.

GOUDHURST, MEASURING THE HOPS 1904 52571
From Victorian times up to the start of the Second World
War, Goudhurst and other Wealden villages among the
hop fields were subjected to an annual late summer
invasion of entire families from South London and
the East End, who supplied the labour force for the
harvesting of the crop. The workers were paid on a piece-
rate, and here the overseer is seen entering the result of
one family's endeavours into his record book.

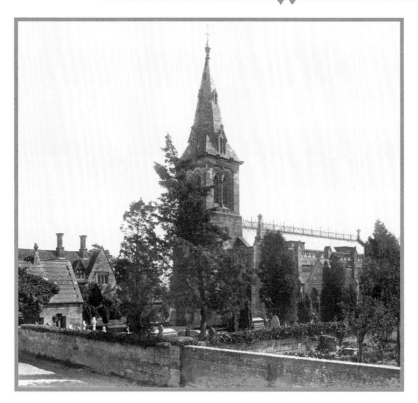

GOUDHURST, KILNDOWN CHURCH 1901

46392

High up on the Sussex border stands this ornate Victorian church, whose building was initiated by Viscount Beresford in 1839, but was then taken on by his twenty-year-old stepson Alexander Beresford Hope. He augmented the stone broach spire with lucarnes, and the length of the church roof with a pierced parapet. Over the ensuing five years he also enriched the interior with a riot of colour, featuring painted wood, stone, glass and tiles. The Beresford family tombs are in the churchyard, overlooked by the gargoyles on the tower and the groups of yew trees.

BIDDENDEN, THE VILLAGE 1901 46456

This is one of the numerous 'dens', or forest clearings, in this part of Kent. The old houses along this main street, some half-timbered, others of brick, or board or tile fronted, were mostly constructed during the 15th century when the village prospered in the profitable cloth trade centred at Cranbrook.

BIDDENDEN, THE VILLAGE 1901 46457
The village is still celebrated on Easter Monday as the home of the Maids of Biddenden, Eliza and Mary Chulkhurst, two Tudor Siamese twins joined at the shoulders and hips, who lived for thirty-four years. When one died, the other declined to be separated, and herself died six hours later.

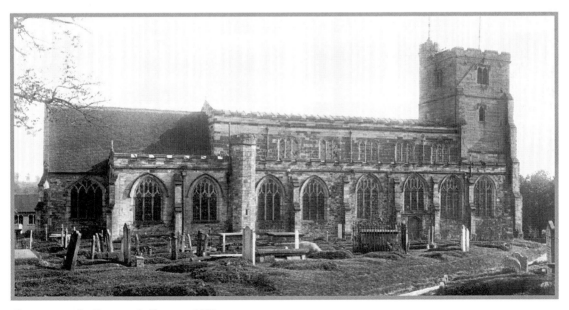

CRANBROOK, ST DUNSTAN'S CHURCH 1901 46439
Dedicated to the local saint, and often called 'the Cathedral of the Weald', it was built of local yellow sandstone in the mid 15th century, and was restored during the 19th century. The south wall of the tower has an impressive clock, with the figure of Father Time, supposedly paid for out of the profits from the parish farm, which was ostensibly operated for the benefit of the unemployed during the Napoleonic wars. Above the porch is a parvise, or priest's room, said to have been used as a prison during the persecutions of Mary Tudor.

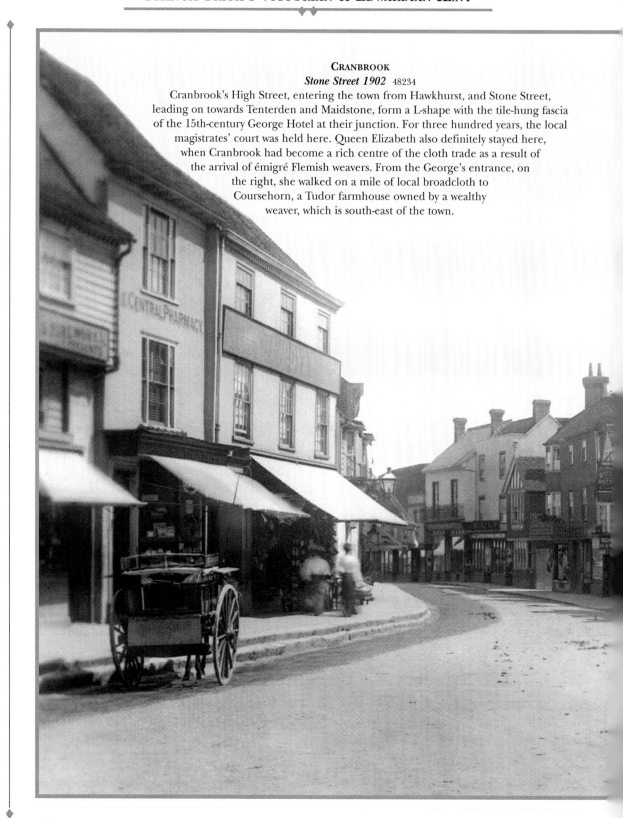

CRANBROOK
Stone Street 1902 48234
Cranbrook's High Street, entering the town from Hawkhurst, and Stone Street,
leading on towards Tenterden and Maidstone, form a L-shape with the tile-hung fascia
of the 15th-century George Hotel at their junction. For three hundred years, the local
magistrates' court was held here. Queen Elizabeth also definitely stayed here,
when Cranbrook had become a rich centre of the cloth trade as a result of
the arrival of émigré Flemish weavers. From the George's entrance, on
the right, she walked on a mile of local broadcloth to
Coursehorn, a Tudor farmhouse owned by a wealthy
weaver, which is south-east of the town.

BENENDEN, THE CHURCH AND THE GREEN 1901 46448

Here we see a Maytime scene of the long, tongue-shaped village green, with the church of St George in the background, and the chestnut trees in full blossom. The green occupies a small place in the annals of cricketing history: it was during a match here that a ball was alleged to have passed between the stumps without removing the bails.

BENENDEN, THE CHURCH 1901 46449

Seen here from the south, across the bank of the small stream which flows through the village, the pale sandstone outline of St George's Church stands proudly in its churchyard. Struck by lightning in 1672, it was restored in 1862 by the architect David Brandon. The battlemented tower with its small pinnacle once sported a quaint timber belfry, which rose to a height of 130 feet.

BENENDEN, THE VILLAGE 1901 46447
A pony and trap stand on the main road which passes by the foot of the green on the left, around which are the tile-hung yeomens' cottages and the village pub. Within two decades, this section of the village was to be augmented by the addition of the large bronze war memorial with its statue depicting Motherhood.

TENTERDEN
High Street 1900 44994
The main body of the church dates back to the
13th and 14th centuries, and was here in 1180. It
is dedicated to the former abbess of Minster, and
in the earliest records Tenterden was part of the
manor of Minster-in-Thanet. The town, a prosperous
agricultural centre, consists mainly of this long street,
with its attractive lines of trees, which widens at its west
end into a picturesque boulevard with grass verges.

TENTERDEN, HIGH STREET 1900 44991

The 15th-century grey tower of St Mildred's Church, with its bold crocketed pinnacles, dominates the centre of this small town, which stands 322 feet above sea level; it was formerly used as a beacon tower in the time of the Spanish Armada. From the top the French coast at Cap Griz Nez can be seen.

TENTERDEN, HIGH STREET 1903 50995

Across the broad expanse of the High Street is the portico of the Town Hall, which was rebuilt in 1790. Adjoining it is the 15th-century Woolpack Inn, where the archbishops are said to have lodged on their brief visits to the town.

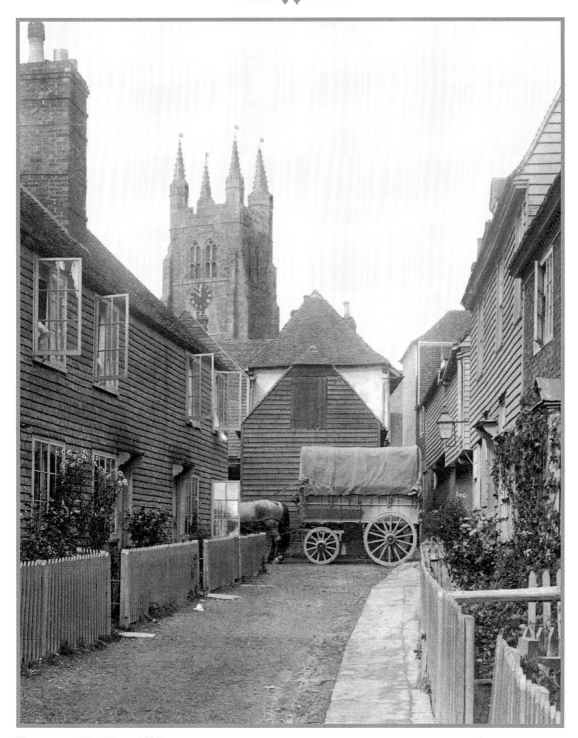

TENTERDEN, THE TOWN 1902 49075
The church tower rises above these small weatherboarded and tiled cottages in a side lane off the main High Street. The narrowness of the thoroughfare must have posed problems for the driver of the horse-drawn wagon seen halted outside the barn at the end.

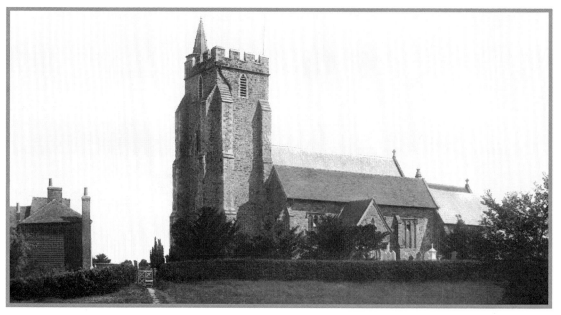

ROLVENDEN, THE CHURCH 1901 46455
The church of St Mary the Virgin, standing on its mound on the edge of Romney Marsh and viewed here from the south-west, dates from the 13th and 15th centuries. Beneath its dark-coloured tower with a crocketed spirelet, it contains one notable oddity: a squire's pew situated at first-floor level over the south chapel, furnished with a carpet, table and Chippendale chairs.

ROLVENDEN, THE VILLAGE 1901 46453
The broad street of the village, with its grass verges, is lined with brick and weatherboarded houses. At one of these cottages lived an elderly lady, who spent much time seated at her window, who as a four-year-old girl had been present at the Battle of Waterloo with her father, a colour sergeant in the army. The wheeled cart in the centre of the picture bears the crest of the Royal Mail.

SMALLHYTHE, THE VILLAGE 1900 45007
The ancient harbour of Tenterden, this was once a shipbuilding centre and was visited by Henry VIII in 1538. The timber-framed yeoman's house in the centre of the picture was built in about 1480 for the harbourmaster, but at the time of this photograph it was the home of the actress Ellen Terry, who lived here until her death in 1928. The half-timbered house on the left was the Priest's House, and it stands beside a small church which was rebuilt in brick after being burned down in 1514.

HAWKHURST, ST LAURENCE'S CHURCH 1902 48258
This 15th-century church built of squared ragstone blocks has a tower 75 feet high standing amid a number of chestnut trees. A defoliated oak tree is supported by a wall which has been constructed to support it. The fine Perpendicular windows have exceptionally beautiful tracery and were added in about 1450, but their glass was shattered by a flying bomb which landed in the churchyard in 1944. After twelve years' restoration, one now commemorates the 19th-century astronomer Sir John Herschel, who lived in the village for the last thirty years of his life.

HAWKHURST, THE COLONNADE 1902 48245

The modern segment of Hawkhurst, known as Highgate, grew up along a section of the A268 during the 18th and 19th centuries. This fairly graceful early 19th-century shopping arcade, with its weatherboarded houses with large shop windows under a colonnade of thin cast iron columns, included a general hardware and implement store, whose proprietor has clearly taken advantage of its protective covering to display an assortment of his wares on the pavement below.

SISSINGHURST, THE CHURCH AND THE SCHOOLS 1902 48238

The red-brick village school with its bell-tower and half-tiled gables was built on the main road between Ashford and Royal Tunbridge Wells during the late 19th century, adjoining the churchyard of Holy Trinity; it was constructed in 1837-8 by the architect J Jennings of Hawkhurst, using squared sandstone blocks.

Index

The Francis Frith Collection Titles

www.francisfrith.co.uk

The Francis Frith Collection publishes over 100 new titles each year. A selection of those currently available is listed below. For latest catalogue please contact The Francis Frith Collection. **Town Books** 96 pages, approximately 75 photos. **County and Themed Books** 128 pages, approximately 135 photos (unless specified). Pocket Albums are miniature editions of Frith local history books 128 pages, approximately 95 photos.

Accrington Old and New
Alderley Edge and Wilmslow
Amersham, Chesham and Rickmansworth
Andover
Around Abergavenny
Around Alton
Aylesbury
Barnstaple
Bedford
Bedfordshire
Berkshire Living Memories
Berkshire Pocket Album
Blackpool Pocket Album
Bognor Regis
Bournemouth
Bradford
Bridgend
Bridport
Brighton and Hove
Bristol
Buckinghamshire
Calne Living Memories
Camberley Pocket Album
Canterbury Cathedral
Cardiff Old and New
Chatham and the Medway Towns
Chelmsford
Chepstow Then and Now
Cheshire
Cheshire Living Memories
Chester
Chesterfield
Chigwell
Christchurch
Churches of East Cornwall
Clevedon
Clitheroe
Corby Living Memories
Cornish Coast
Cornwall Living Memories
Cotswold Living Memories
Cotswold Pocket Album
Coulsdon, Chipstead and Woodmanstern
County Durham
Cromer, Sheringham and Holt
Dartmoor Pocket Album
Derby
Derbyshire
Derbyshire Living Memories
Devon
Devon Churches
Dorchester

Dorset Coast Pocket Album
Dorset Living Memories
Dorset Villages
Down the Dart
Down the Severn
Down the Thames
Dunmow, Thaxted and Finchingfield
Durham
East Anglia Pocket Album
East Devon
East Grinstead
Edinburgh
Ely and The Fens
Essex Pocket Album
Essex Second Selection
Essex: The London Boroughs
Exeter
Exmoor
Falmouth
Farnborough, Fleet and Aldershot
Folkestone
Frome
Furness and Cartmel Peninsulas
Glamorgan
Glasgow
Glastonbury
Gloucester
Gloucestershire
Greater Manchester
Guildford
Hailsham
Hampshire
Harrogate
Hastings and Bexhill
Haywards Heath Living Memories
Heads of the Valleys
Heart of Lancashire Pocket Album
Helston
Herefordshire
Horsham
Humberside Pocket Album
Huntingdon, St Neots and St Ives
Hythe, Romney Marsh and Ashford
Ilfracombe
Ipswich Pocket Album
Isle of Wight
Isle of Wight Living Memories
King's Lynn
Kingston upon Thames
Lake District Pocket Album
Lancashire Living Memories
Lancashire Villages

Available from your local bookshop or from the publisher

The Francis Frith Collection Titles (continued)

Lancaster, Morecambe and Heysham Pocket Album
Leeds Pocket Album
Leicester
Leicestershire
Lincolnshire Living Memoires
Lincolnshire Pocket Album
Liverpool and Merseyside
London Pocket Album
Ludlow
Maidenhead
Maidstone
Malmesbury
Manchester Pocket Album
Marlborough
Matlock
Merseyside Living Memories
Nantwich and Crewe
New Forest
Newbury Living Memories
Newquay to St Ives
North Devon Living Memories
North London
North Wales
North Yorkshire
Northamptonshire
Northumberland
Northwich
Nottingham
Nottinghamshire Pocket Album
Oakham
Odiham Then and Now
Oxford Pocket Album
Oxfordshire
Padstow
Pembrokeshire
Penzance
Petersfield Then and Now
Plymouth
Poole and Sandbanks
Preston Pocket Album
Ramsgate Old and New
Reading Pocket Album
Redditch Living Memories
Redhill to Reigate
Richmond
Ringwood
Rochdale
Romford Pocket Album
Salisbury Pocket Album
Scotland
Scottish Castles
Sevenoaks and Tonbridge
Sheffield and South Yorkshire Pocket Album
Shropshire
Somerset
South Devon Coast
South Devon Living Memories
South East London
Southampton Pocket Album
Southend Pocket Album
Southport

Southwold to Aldeburgh
Stourbridge Living Memories
Stratford upon Avon
Stroud
Suffolk
Suffolk Pocket Album
Surrey Living Memories
Sussex
Sutton
Swanage and Purbeck
Swansea Pocket Album
Swindon Living Memories
Taunton
Teignmouth
Tenby and Saundersfoot
Tiverton
Torbay
Truro
Uppingham
Villages of Kent
Villages of Surrey
Villages of Sussex Pocket Album
Wakefield and the Five Towns Living Memories
Warrington
Warwick
Warwickshire Pocket Album
Wellingborough Living Memories
Wells
Welsh Castles
West Midlands Pocket Album
West Wiltshire Towns
West Yorkshire
Weston-super-Mare
Weymouth
Widnes and Runcorn
Wiltshire Churches
Wiltshire Living Memories
Wiltshire Pocket Album
Wimborne
Winchester Pocket Album
Windermere
Windsor
Wirral
Wokingham and Bracknell
Woodbridge
Worcester
Worcestershire
Worcestershire Living Memories
Wyre Forest
York Pocket Album
Yorkshire
Yorkshire Coastal Memories
Yorkshire Dales
Yorkshire Revisited

See Frith books on the internet at www.francisfrith.co.uk

FRITH PRODUCTS & SERVICES

Francis Frith would doubtless be pleased to know that the pioneering publishing venture he started in 1860 still continues today. Over a hundred and forty years later, The Francis Frith Collection continues in the same innovative tradition and is now one of the foremost publishers of vintage photographs in the world. Some of the current activities include:

Interior Decoration

Today Frith's photographs can be seen framed and as giant wall murals in thousands of pubs, restaurants, hotels, banks, retail stores and other public buildings throughout the country. In every case they enhance the unique local atmosphere of the places they depict and provide reminders of gentler days in an increasingly busy and frenetic world.

Product Promotions

Frith products are used by many major companies to promote the sales of their own products or to reinforce their own history and heritage. Frith promotions have been used by Hovis bread, Courage beers, Scots Porage Oats, Colman's mustard, Cadbury's foods, Mellow Birds coffee, Dunhill pipe tobacco, Guinness, and Bulmer's Cider.

Genealogy and Family History

As the interest in family history and roots grows world-wide, more and more people are turning to Frith's photographs of Great Britain for images of the towns, villages and streets where their ancestors lived; and, of course, photographs of the churches and chapels where their ancestors were christened, married and buried are an essential part of every genealogy tree and family album.

Frith Products

All Frith photographs are available Framed or just as Mounted Prints and Posters (size 23 x 16 inches). These may be ordered from the address below. From time to time other products - Address Books, Calendars, Table Mats, etc - are available.

The Internet

Already ninety thousand Frith photographs can be viewed and purchased on the internet through the Frith websites and a myriad of partner sites.

For more detailed information on Frith companies and products, look at these sites:

www.francisfrith.co.uk
www.francisfrith.com
(for North American visitors)

See the complete list of Frith Books at:
www.francisfrith.co.uk
This web site is regularly updated with the latest list of publications from The Francis Frith Collection. If you wish to buy books relating to another part of the country that your local bookshop does not stock, you may purchase on-line.

For further information, trade, or author enquiries please contact us at the address below:
The Francis Frith Collection, Frith's Barn, Teffont, Salisbury, Wiltshire, England SP3 5QP.
Tel: +44 (0)1722 716 376 Fax: +44 (0)1722 716 881 Email: sales@francisfrith.co.uk

See Frith books on the internet at www.francisfrith.co.uk

FREE PRINT OF YOUR CHOICE

Mounted Print
Overall size 14 x 11 inches (355 x 280mm)

Choose any Frith photograph in this book.
Simply complete the Voucher opposite and return it with your remittance for £3.50 (to cover postage and handling) and we will print the photograph of your choice in SEPIA (size 11 x 8 inches) and supply it in a cream mount with a burgundy rule line (overall size 14 x 11 inches).
Please note: photographs with a reference number starting with a "Z" are not Frith photographs and cannot be supplied under this offer.
Offer valid for delivery to one UK address only.

PLUS: **Order additional Mounted Prints at HALF PRICE - £7.49 each** (normally £14.99)
If you would like to order more Frith prints from this book, possibly as gifts for friends and family, you can buy them at half price (with no additional postage and handling costs).

PLUS: **Have your Mounted Prints framed**
For an extra £14.95 per print you can have your mounted print(s) framed in an elegant polished wood and gilt moulding, overall size 16 x 13 inches (no additional postage and handling required).

IMPORTANT!

These special prices are only available if you use this form to order. You must use the ORIGINAL VOUCHER on this page (no copies permitted). We can only despatch to one UK address. This offer cannot be combined with any other offer.

Send completed Voucher form to:
The Francis Frith Collection, Frith's Barn, Teffont, Salisbury, Wiltshire SP3 5QP

CHOOSE A PHOTOGRAPH FROM THIS BOOK

Voucher for *FREE* and Reduced Price *Frith Prints*

Please do not photocopy this voucher. Only the original is valid, so please fill it in, cut it out and return it to us with your order.

Picture ref no	Page no	Qty	Mounted @ £7.49	Framed + £14.95	Total Cost £
		1	Free of charge*	£	£
			£7.49	£	£
			£7.49	£	£
			£7.49	£	£
			£7.49	£	£
			£7.49	£	£

Please allow 28 days for delivery. Offer available to one UK address only

* Post & handling	£3.50
Total Order Cost	£

Title of this book . . . .

I enclose a cheque/postal order for £ . . . .
made payable to 'The Francis Frith Collection'

OR please debit my Mastercard / Visa / Maestro card, details below

Card Number

Issue No (Maestro only)   Valid from (Maestro)

Expires   Signature

Name Mr/Mrs/Ms . . . .

Address . . . .
. . . .
. . . .
. . . . Postcode . . . .

Daytime Tel No . . . .

Email . . . .

ISBN 1-85937-624-X   Valid to 31/12/08

Free Print – see overleaf

Can you help us with information about any of the Frith photographs in this book?

We are gradually compiling an historical record for each of the photographs in the Frith archive. It is always fascinating to find out the names of the people shown in the pictures, as well as insights into the shops, buildings and other features depicted.

If you recognize anyone in the photographs in this book, or if you have information not already included in the author's caption, do let us know. We would love to hear from you, and will try to publish it in future books or articles.

Our production team

Frith books are produced by a small dedicated team at offices in the converted Grade II listed 18th-century barn at Teffont near Salisbury, illustrated above. Most have worked with The Francis Frith Collection for many years. All have in common one quality: they have a passion for The Francis Frith Collection. The team is constantly expanding, but currently includes:

Andrew Alsop, Paul Baron, Jason Buck, John Buck, Jenny Coles, Heather Crisp, David Davies, Natalie Davis, Louis du Mont, Isobel Hall, Chris Hardwick, Julian Hight, Peter Horne, James Kinnear, Karen Kinnear, Tina Leary, Stuart Login, Sue Molloy, Sarah Roberts, Kate Rotondetto, Eliza Sackett, Terence Sackett, Sandra Sampson, Adrian Sanders, Sandra Sanger, Julia Skinner, Lewis Taylor, Will Tunnicliffe, David Turner and Ricky Williams.